The F-14 Tomcat

TERRY C. TREADWELL

AMBERLEY

First published 2019

Amberley Publishing
The Hill, Stroud,
Gloucestershire, GL5 4EP

www.amberley-books.com

ISBN 978 1 4456 8639 4 (print)
ISBN 978 1 4456 8640 0 (ebook)

British Library Cataloguing in Publication Data.
A catalogue record for this book is available from the British Library.

Typeset in 10pt on 12pt Celeste.
Typesetting by Aura Technology and Software Services, India.
Printed in the UK.

Contents

Introduction

The design philosophy for the Grumman F-14 Tomcat actually began to take shape back in the late 1950s when it was realised that the Russians were quickly developing an increasingly accurate airborne missile system. The Navy, concerned that such a capability would render their ships vulnerable to long-distance air strikes, proposed a program called Fleet Air Defence (FAD) and Douglas Aircraft produced a design for an aircraft called the F-6D Missileer. It was designed to be nothing more than a launch platform for Bendix XAAM-M-10 'Eagle' missiles and was to have a stand-off and loiter capability. The Bendix missile was capable of reaching Mach 4 and had a range of over 150 miles. After a great deal of research it was decided that the F-6D Missileer's overall combat capability was far too limited and the programme was cancelled.

In 1962, the Secretary of Defence, Robert McNamara, wanted to create a multi-service aircraft that could be used by both the Navy and the Air Force under the umbrella of the Tactical Fighter Experimental (TFX) programme. The result was the F-111A/B: A for the Air Force, B for the Navy. It was to be the first variable swing aircraft; the first to incorporate an afterburning turbofan engine, have an encapsulated ejection system, have the capability to fly intentionally at sea level at supersonic speed; and to incorporate a dedicated terrain following radar system. The Navy saw no future for the F-111B as an aircraft operating from an aircraft carrier, and Vice-Admiral Tom Connolly, who was DCNO at the time, voiced his objections to the Senate committee in no uncertain manner when asked for his opinion, which resulted in the demise of the F-111B. It was also to be the aircraft that prevented Vice-Admiral Thomas F. Connolly getting his fourth star.

The Navy issued an RFP (Request For Proposals) with the requirements of a two-man crew in tandem, two engines, the ability to carry a long-range advanced missile weapons system, an advanced radar and to have the ability to land on an aircraft carrier with full armament and a minimum fuel load. Of the five companies that tendered for the project, Grumman emerged the choice of the Navy. The F-14 was the result for a shipborne fighter (VFX) and coming from a long line of successful Grumman 'Cat' aircraft built for the Navy (the F4 Wildcat, F6 Hellcat, F7 Tigercat and F8 Bearcat), the F-14 Tomcat seemed a natural progression. There were six design proposals – 303A, B, C, D, E and F – before 303G was selected. The development of this supersonic aircraft came about after the major disagreement between the US Navy and the Secretary of Defence, Robert McNamara, and the F-14 Tomcat was to become one of the most sophisticated, reliable and deadly aircraft of its day.

The first test flight of the F-14 was uneventful, but the second test flight of the F-14 is covered together with a unique photograph of the two pilots, Chief Test Pilot Bob Smyth and Project Test Pilot Bill Miller, ejecting from the aircraft after a major hydraulic failure.

The operational career of the F-14, which began in September 1974 with the VF-1 (Wolfpack) and VF-2 (Bounty Hunters) squadrons operating from the aircraft carrier USS *Enterprise* (CVN-65), is covered. Also covered is the part played by the F-14 Tomcat during the Iraqi War and Desert Storm, and its unique experience in successfully shooting down Russian-built fighter aircraft in dogfights.

The F-14 Tomcat carried a formidable amount of firepower, which included a Vulcan M-61 A1 20 mm cannon for close-in combat, with 675 rounds of ammunition, and AIM-9 Sidewinder heat-seeking missiles. Moreover, it the only fighter capable of carrying the AIM-54 Phoenix missiles.

There are about 150 photographs of the F-14 in this book, including those in Iranian livery that were ordered before the Shah of Iran was deposed by the revolutionaries. There is also a unique photograph showing the successful ejection of the F-14 crew during the second test flight. This is not the definitive work on this aircraft, but it will give the reader an insight into one of the most iconic aircraft of its day.

Terry Treadwell

An F-14 Tomcats of VF-1 (Wolfpack) being hoisted aboard the aircraft carrier USS *Enterprise* (CVN-65).

Chapter One

In 1942, Dr Alexander Lippisch, an aerodynamicist for the German aircraft manufacturer Messerschmitt, patented a design for a swept-wing aircraft. In Britain, Barnes Wallis, designer of the R101 airship, the Wellington bomber and the 'Bouncing Bomb' that destroyed the Mohne and Eder Dams during the Second World War, was carrying out experiments with models on just the same thing. Some years later, during the 1950s, Barnes Wallis designed a supersonic airliner with variable sweep wings that swung back against the fuselage called the Swallow. The design of the Vickers Swallow placed the engines toward the wingtips, the idea being that it would produce a centre of gravity movement to match the aerodynamic centre, thus keeping the longitudinal stability reasonably constant. A design model was taken to the wind tunnel facility at the NACA's (National Advisory Committee for Aeronautics) Langley Field, where after extensive tests it was decided that the concept of wingtip-mounted engines was impractical. The design progressed no farther and was scrapped.

The NACA (later to become NASA – National Air and Space Administration) continued to carry out wind tunnel experiments on the design, and with the aid of a computer discovered that by careful positioning of the hinge away from the fuselage, the wings as

Above: A model of the Vickers Swallow.

Left: Aerial shot of the Mohne Dam after being breached.

they swept aft did not produce excessive stability supersonically. This ensured that the longitudinal stability remained within the bounds of acceptability.

Also in the 1950s, across the Atlantic Ocean, the Bell Aircraft Corporation successfully built and flew their swing-wing aircraft, the Bell X-5. The X-5 was based on a captured German design, the Messerschmitt P.1101, which was given to the Bell Aircraft Corporation for examination after the war. The German Messerschmitt P.1101 had ground-adjustable variable sweep wings, while the Bell X-5 had an in-flight variable sweep capability. Late in 1952, Grumman designed and built a swing-wing fighter called the XF10F-1 Jaguar and in May 1953, using all the information that it had gleaned from the test flights of the Bell X-5, it took to the air. Design studies had also been carried out of the Bell X-5 by the NACA and because of this, the US Navy saw a great potential in Grumman's swing-wing fighter and ordered ten. But, as with a lot of great ideas, sometimes the concept is ahead of its time and materials and engines are not capable of matching the enthusiasm. Only one of the XF10F-1 Jaguars was ever built and the orders for the remaining nine were cancelled, much to the relief of some of the Grumman engineers. A replacement was urgently required for the aging Douglas F-3H Demon and the short-legged F-4D Skyray (later to become the F-6A Skyray), which were the US Navy's principal fighter aircraft.

Interest in a new fighter began late in the 1950s, following reports on the latest Russian fighters, the Tupolev Tu-28 Fiddler and the Mikoyan Gurevich (MiG)-21D Fishbed. The US Navy decided that they required a subsonic fighter capable of delivering multiple missiles at a large number of targets. The aircraft they decided on was a 'paper' aeroplane called the

A Messerschmitt P.1101, seen in a front three-quarter view.

The Bell X-5, based on the design of the Messerschmitt P.1101.

The X-F10F making its first public appearance.

A front three-quarter view of the XF10F.

Above: The X-F10F taking off on its initial test flight.

Right: The McDonnell/ Douglas F-3H-2N on a test flight.

The Douglas F-4D Skyray, which would later become the F-6A Skyray.

Above: Tupolev Tu-128

Left: An excellent shot of the MiG-21 in flight.

A MiG-21 about to take off.

A MiG-21 of the Czech Air Force.

Douglas F-6D Missileer. The F-6D was designed to carry the Grumman two-stage XAAM-10 Eagle missile, a track-while-scan missile control system, an active homing radar guidance system, and a high-powered pulse Doppler system. It had a straight wing, on which six Eagle missiles could be externally mounted. Two newly designed Pratt & Whitney TF30-P-2 engines were chosen for the F-6D, and Grumman were in charge of designing and developing the missile. The project never got past the design stage before it was cancelled by the then Secretary of Defence, Robert McNamara. He had decided that the cost was too high considering that the aircraft could only perform one role. A multi-role, combat aircraft was what was really required.

The Navy continued to look around after the cancellation of the Douglas Missileer, so McNamara suggested that the US Navy and the US Air Force combine their requirements and select one aircraft. The aircraft chosen was the General Dynamics F-111A, a variable swing-wing aircraft designed primarily for the USAF as a low-level interceptor. This was just the type of aircraft that General F. F. Everest, the USAF's Tactical Air Command's new commander, wanted. He required an aircraft to replace the F-105, one that could fly non-stop to Europe without refuelling, fly at low level at 1,000 mph for 400 miles, and at high level at 1,700 mph. From the outset it was obvious that the requirements of both services were poles apart. The pressure on them to combine their needs continued, so the US Navy asked Grumman to join with General Dynamics and make a naval version of the F-111A with longer wings and an armament of six Hughes AIM-54A (Air Interceptor Missile) Phoenix missiles with the AWG-9 weapon system. It was called the F-111B (TFX).

Although the F-111B (nicknamed the Sea Pig by the Naval and test flight crews) was built for the Navy, the programme as a whole was run by the USAF. The F-111B's initial flight was on 18 May 1966 and, almost immediately, there were problems – the major one being weight. The Navy had estimated the F-111B's desired weight to be around 60,000 lbs

A model of the TF-30 Missileer showing six Eagle missiles beneath the wings.

Left: USAF EF-111A.

Below: Plan drawing of the 303E.

Design 303E

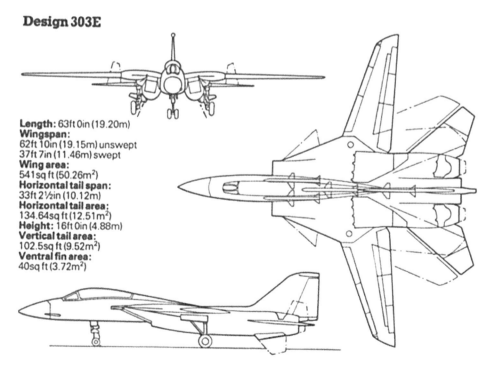

Length: 63ft 0in (19.20m)
Wingspan:
62ft 10in (19.15m) unswept
37ft 7in (11.46m) swept
Wing area:
541sq ft (50.26m^2)
Horizontal tail span:
33ft 2½in (10.12m)
Horizontal tail area:
134.64sq ft (12.51m^2)
Height: 16ft 0in (4.88m)
Vertical tail area:
102.5sq ft (9.52m^2)
Ventral fin area:
40sq ft (3.72m^2)

An F-111A, with the Phoenix missile system logo on the tail, at Hughes Aircraft Co.

Above: Another shot of an F-111A at Hughes Aircraft Co.

Right: A Navy F-111B on its maiden flight from the Grumman facility at Calverton, New York.

mark; in reality, the weight of the F-111B was in excess of 70,000 lbs. Although this was acceptable to the Air Force, it was not to the Navy, and essentially killed any chance of the aircraft being accepted as a carrier aircraft. It was obvious that this weight would probably increase during development, and this was totally unacceptable to the Navy. McNamara insisted that the engine be upgraded to handle the increased weight, and out of this engine modification came the Pratt & Whitney TF30-P-412, which later became the engine for the F-14 Tomcat. Problems were being experienced in certain areas of the flying envelope. Among other things, the engine inlets were causing compressor stalls. Pilots were also complaining about the lack of visibility on approach to carriers due to the angle of attack, and serious reflection problems were caused by the angle of the windshield.

McNamara, who by this time was at the point of despairing over the project, called together all the top executives of the companies involved for twice-monthly meetings. He had even hired his own project engineer, Bob Laidlaw, from North American/Rockwell, to supervise the meetings and be his own personal consultant. These meetings were held in Washington on Saturday mornings and included the Secretaries of the Navy and the Air Force. They tried unsuccessfully to solve their differences and the problems that were dogging the project. Among the Navy contingent at the meetings were Admiral Thomas Moorer, Chief of Naval Operations (CNO), and Vice-Admiral Thomas F. Connolly, Deputy Chief of Naval Operations (DCNO), and although they and the Navy realised that as far as they were concerned the project was a `no-go', the Secretary of Defence did not, and pushed on with the project.

The reason for building a 'swing-wing' aircraft as we know was not new, but the main reason was relatively simple: it lets aircraft go faster by reducing the drag created by air pressure. If you put your arm straight out of the window of your car as it is travelling along and then bend your arm to right angles, the drag resistance is reduced dramatically. There are two different types of drag: parasite drag and induced drag. Parasite drag increases as the speed increases. If the speed is doubled, then the parasite drag is quadrupled; halve the speed and the drag is reduced by just one quarter. Create a swing-wing and some of that drag is reduced noticeably.

Induced drag is associated with lift and is the other main contributor to the whole drag equation. In the case of an aircraft, when a wing goes through the air it disrupts the airstream in front of it, known as the local airstream, and it is this that induces the drag. Remote free airstream is the air furthest away from the aircraft. To get the relative wind to come straight across the wing, the wing had to increase its angle of attack by retracting the wings to 68 degrees. By doing this it increased the lifting force back slightly. With the swing-wing extended, it will have a higher aspect ratio and create less induced drag; with the swing-wing retracted to 68 degrees, it will have a lower aspect ratio and will create more induced drag.

The swing-wing was one of the innovations developed for the F-111B, but during the wind tunnel tests the pivot points were discovered to be causing problems: they reduced the cross-sectional area and the fuel flow in low altitude supersonic flight. Nothing seemed to be going right for the project. The aircraft was required to fly at supersonic speeds at low altitude, utilising the latest terrain-following radar, and to carry the extremely heavy Phoenix missile system, with its multi-shot capability at high altitudes. To enable the aircraft to do this, its drag had to be reduced drastically, so the wing pivots were located inboard and the engines pulled into the fuselage at the wing roots, instead of being outboard under each wing. This too created problems with the airflow and cut engine efficiency tremendously. To put the whole project into its correct perspective, as a land-based bomber it would be adequate, but as a fighter or interceptor it would be no good at all.

Admiral Connolly decided to go down to Fort Worth, Texas, where the F-111B was being tested, to see for himself what the aircraft was like. He flew the aircraft accompanied by

An F-111B, the Navy version of the Air Force F-111A.

A Navy F-111B showing a partial swept-wing configuration. The pilot seems to wearing a full 'space type' helmet, suggesting a high-altitude test.

an Air Force pilot and agreed that for Air Force use it had great potential, but for use by the Navy and to fly off aircraft carriers it had none. Up to this point, there had been six variations, and a decision on which was to be the prime aircraft still had to be made. The R&D (Research and Development) costs were climbing all the time. In 1966, $250 million was injected into the budget, and it was obvious to all concerned that this was to be the year of decision, as all previous assessments had only been in the region of $30 and $40 million.

Admiral Moorer, as Chief of Naval Operations, was in charge of requirements for the Navy at this time and it was his job to decide what the Navy should or should not have. It was also his decision that the Navy did not want the F-111B. In the meantime, he was getting feedback information from the test pilots carrying out the trials at Patuxent River Naval Air Test Centre that the F-111B could in no way successfully operate off an aircraft carrier. It was unstable to the point of being dangerous, and this was totally unacceptable, especially when being flown in adverse weather conditions. But still the civilian hierarchy insisted that the Navy accept the F-111B. It was around this time that Grumman made an unsolicited approach to the Navy with their concept of a new fighter, the F-14. Grumman was already involved with the F-111B as sub-contractor, building the aircraft's aft section for General Dynamics, but they realised that it was not suitable as a carrier aircraft, so had come up with a proposal of their own. The Navy looked at the proposal very carefully and realised that it could be the answer to all their problems. The design took in the best features of the F-111B and placed them in a brand-new airframe; what was even more

An F-111B about to land at Calverton after a test flight.

important, the R&D had already been done on the engine and weapon systems. All that had to be tested was the new airframe and that was the cheapest part of all. All this gave the Navy an alternative proposal when they pushed for the cancellation of the F-111B programme. A comparison study was made between the F-14, the F-111 and a couple of other aircraft. The results showed that the F-14 was a far better aircraft than any of the others, but still Secretary of Defence NcMamara pushed for the F-111B.

Admiral Moorer was summoned to the Secretary of the Navy's office and asked if he would back the F-111B project and again the Admiral said 'No!' The Navy realised that they were getting nowhere with their objections and so decided to take advantage of the Senate Preparedness Sub-Committee's offer of help. A hearing was held, chaired by Senator Stennis, who was also the Chairman of the Senate Armed Services Committee, and he wanted a good reason why his committee should disapprove the $20 million for the project.

Paul Ignatius, the new Secretary of the Navy, Assistant Secretary of the Navy for Research and Development Bob Frosch, Chief of Naval Operations Admiral Thomas Moorer, Deputy Chief of Naval Operations Vice-Admiral Thomas F. Connolly and Rear Admiral Gerry Miller, who represented the Department of Defence, were summoned. For over six hours Stennis asked questions and Paul Ignatius answered them, and it was quite obvious that nothing concrete was going to be said regarding the future of the F-111B project.

It was at this point that Rear Admiral Miller, who had been working closely with Stennis's right-hand man, left the room. Five minutes later one of Stennis's aides entered the room and placed a note in front of Stennis. Stennis barely glanced at it, asked a couple of innocuous questions, and then said, 'This question is for Admiral Connolly; he is the Air Boss for the Navy and this is his area of responsibility. Admiral, would you support this additional money for the F-111B?'

Admiral Connolly looked at Stennis and replied, 'No sir, I would not.'

The Secretary of the Navy, Paul Ignatius, immediately said, 'Well we are going to put better engines in the aircraft and make a better airplane out of it.'

Stennis turned back to Admiral Connolly and said, 'Admiral, with the new engines would you change your mind?'

Admiral Connolly took a deep breath, looked directly at Stennis and said, 'Senator, there isn't enough thrust in all Christendom to make a Navy fighter out of that airplane.'

Although the F-111B project was dead as far as the Navy was concerned, problems regarding the funding for the F-14 project began to raise their heads. Admiral Zumwalt was still head of the study group for the F-111B and he decided to push for $96 million of the budget to be channelled into the F-111B project, in case the F-14 project folded. The 'Hedge', as it was known, was approved by Admiral Moorer and was the point of discussion when the House Armed Services Committee met. Again, the person in the 'hot seat' at the meeting was Vice-Admiral Connolly, and when asked by the chairman, Mendel Rivers, if he had anything good to say about the F-111B, Admiral Connolly replied: 'Mr Chairman, I don't know of any aviator, reserve or regular, anywhere in the world, who has anything good to say about that airplane!'

That, to all intents and purposes, was the end of the F-111B and also the end of Tom Connolly's hopes of promotion to four-star Admiral.

Chapter Two

Grumman sensed that a cancellation of the F-111B project was likely, and so began a series of project studies of alternative fighters, still using the Pratt & Whitney TF30 engines and AWG-9 avionics system. In October 1967, Grumman proposed a design called the 303-60 to the US Navy, and in May the following year the F-111B project was officially cancelled.

Two months later, the US Navy invited proposals for a new fighter to be submitted, designating it the VFX. In 1968 the F-14 program was born with the Navy's proposal for the VFX (Navy Fighter Experimental) and resulted in Grumman's general design 303. The VFX required a fighter with a two-man crew with tandem seating, two engines, an advanced weapon system with powerful radar plus the ability to carry a variety of long-, medium- and short-range high-performance air-to-air missiles and an internal gun. Furthermore, the VFX should be able to land on an aircraft carrier with a full armament load. Of all the designs and proposals submitted, only one had a fixed wing, all the others having variable swing-wings. It was made known that the aircraft would be purchased in two stages – the VFX-1 with the TF30 engines and later the VFX-2 with the Advanced Technology Engine (ATE), then currently under joint development by the US Navy and the USAF. Two companies were chosen to resubmit designs to the Naval Air Systems Command, Grumman and McDonnell-Douglas. One month later, in October 1968, it was

A model of the proposed F-14 design, VFX-1C.

announced that Grumman had been selected as the prime contractor for the Navy's new fighter aircraft. Certain conditions were laid down by the Navy regarding the design of the aircraft, however, such as the two-man crew being carried in tandem and not side-by-side as in the F-111B, and it also had to be powered by two Pratt & Whitney TF3C-P-412 engines. Its armament was to be six Phoenix missiles, or six AIM-7 Sparrow missiles with two AIM-9 Sidewinders and an internally mounted M-61 rotary cannon. All in all, the aircraft was to be the most sophisticated and lethal fighter in the world.

The contract for the F-14A RDT&E (Research, Development, Test and Evaluation) was signed on 3 February 1969, and less than two years later this remarkable aircraft took off on its maiden flight. The F-14A was the most complicated project ever undertaken by Grumman, although the Lunar Module was to come close. The aircraft was to be the product of 6,000 configurations, culminating in eight different designs: 303-60, 303A, 303B, 303C, 303D, 303E, 303F and 303G. Starting with 303-60, this design had podded engines and a high variable sweep wing. This being the first of the designs, it did not contain the sophisticated blend of electronics and airframe subsystems that subsequent models did. Grumman carried out extensive tests in the wind tunnel, with the result that some slight modifications were made – enough to change the design number to 303A. Modification of the nacelles resulted in the design number being changed yet again, to 303B. Design number 303C was to produce the twin vertical tails that were to be in the final design, and had the engines built into the fuselage, rather than in separate pods. The variable geometric wings were set high on the fuselage, unlike design 303D,

A model of proposed F-14 design 303-0.

A model of the proposed fixed-wing F-14.

Proposed models of 'swing-wing' and 'fixed wing' F-14s.

which, although retaining the engines built into the fuselage and the twin vertical tails, had a low variable geometric wing. The 303E was a variation of the 303B, but with a reduction of 4,920 lbs in overall weight. The 303F was similar to the 303D, the only difference, but an important one, being that it had a fixed wing. The next design, the 303G, had the podded engines and the high-set variable geometric wing, but this design had a fighter-only capability, the weaponry consisting of the AWG-10 fire control system and four Sparrow missiles, but no provision for the Phoenix missile. This was one of the main reasons why the design was dropped. Poor subsonic drag, reduced maximum afterburner supersonic thrust and poor subsonic longitudinal stability were among the reasons why design number 303D was dropped. This left only 303E, B, C and F. Both B and C had the high geometric wing, but C had the engines built into the fuselage and B had the podded engines. C was discarded because of poor subsonic combat performance, inferior fuel flow and afterburner thrust. It also had no potential for ATE engines, and its take-off weight would have been 4,920 lbs heavier for the Sparrow fighter mission than the 303E. B was discarded because of the high wing, and F because of the fixed wing. The only design left was the 303E, which was ultimately chosen to become the F-14 Tomcat. The name 'Tomcat' was given to the aircraft in line with the names given to previous fighters built by Grumman: e.g. Wildcat, Hellcat, Tigercat, and Bearcat etc. It was also said, and widely accepted, to be named after Vice Admiral 'Tom' Connolly, who gave the aircraft so much support, but this has never been officially recognised.

Grumman realised that they were taking a chance by using titanium, because although it is stronger and lighter than steel, it is difficult to work with. Even the usually simple task of drilling holes took on a completely new perspective. The area to be drilled had to be completely submerged in Freon gas to chill the metal, otherwise the drill bit heated the area to a point where the titanium became brittle and lost its strength. Holes had to be drilled precisely and a computerised drill was used to ensure that they were. The rivets were made slightly larger than the holes and were pushed in with such force and accuracy that it caused the two metals to fuse together, thus eliminating the need for a sealant. The rest of the F-14 was made up of approximately 40 per cent aluminium alloy, 18 per cent steel and less than 1 per cent boron.

The F-14A prototype first flew on 21 December 1970, without incident, but on the second, there was a complete loss of the hydraulics and both pilots, Chief Test Pilot Robert Smythe and Project Test Pilot William Miller, had to eject to safety. The cause was pinpointed to a

Above: A full mock-up of the F-14A Tomcat.

Right: An F-14 with its wings extended.

A prototype F-14 on its second flight. This was the replacement aircraft after the crash of the first prototype.

A prototype F-14 on a test flight.

Above: Grumman test pilots Bob Smythe and Bill Miller parachuting to safety after ejecting from their F-14 on its second test flight.

Left: The three stages of the F-14 'swing wing' in flight.

failure in the titanium hydraulic piping due to fatigue. The second F-14A flew five months later, with the titanium piping having been replaced by stainless steel.

The construction of the F-14 was a revolution in aircraft manufacture. Approximately 25 per cent of the aircraft was made of titanium, the majority being in the box beam to which the wings were attached. The box beam had a dual role; not only did it absorb all the transmitted wing loads, but it was also used as a fuel tank. A new technique was used to weld the beam: electron-beam welding, wherein two pieces of titanium were welded into their molecular components, resulting in a strength loss of only 3 per cent. This was well within the acceptable safety margins. All in all, fourteen aircraft were used for the development program, twelve of them instrumented. Two were used for the development of the Hughes Phoenix Missile System at Hughes Aircraft Corporation at Point Mugu, CA. Six were used for airframe/engine testing at the Grumman facilities at Calverton, NY, and four for avionic system development at Point Mugu. Five F-14s (of the six 'airframe' aircraft) spent some time at Patuxent River, Maryland, for carrier suitability trials and for structural, powerplant and performance demonstrations.

The fully proven F-14 was introduced to the fleet only fifty-one months after the contract was awarded! The strength of the titanium and the electron-beam welding was proven when the first pre-production F-14A crashed on 30 December 1970 and the wing-box was found 6 feet underground, virtually undamaged.

Right: An F-14 of VF-213 (Black Lions) seen launching from the angled deck of the USS *Theodore Roosevelt* (CVN-71).

Below: F-14s of VF-31 and VF-213 performing a flypast of the USS *Theodore Roosevelt* (CVN-71).

An excellent shot of an F-14 with its wings swept back.

F-14A test aircraft No. 11 undergoing carrier deck trials aboard the aircraft carrier USS *Independence* (CVL-22).

The following are how the prototypes were used:

Bu. No. 157981: Second prototype used for low-speed handling tests.
Bu. No. 157982: Third prototype used for non-destructive structural tests.
Bu. No. 157983: Fourth prototype was the first F-14 with AN/AWG-9, used for AIM-54 evaluation.
Bu. No. 157984: Fifth prototype used to demonstrate systems compatibility.
Bu. No. 157985: Sixth prototype: Missile separation and weapons separation tests. Crashed on 20 June 1973 and was lost near Point Mugu when an AIM-7 pitched up on launch and ruptured a fuel tank, causing a fire which necessitated crew ejection.
Bu. No. 157986: Seventh prototype used as engine test bed, later used as F-14B-30GR prototype and then modified as F-14A (+) prototype.
Bu. No. 157987: Eighth prototype for Navy evaluation tests. Aircraft crashed on 13 May 1974 after suffering an engine fire on ground at Patuxent River.
Bu. No. 157988: Ninth prototype for AN/AWG-9 evaluation.
Bu. No. 157989: Tenth prototype used for carrier qualification evaluation. Aircraft crashed on 30 June 1972 near Chesapeake Bay while practising for an air show at Patuxent River.
Bu. No. 157990: Eleventh prototype used for non-weapons systems avionics tests
Bu. No. 157991: Twelfth prototype (re-designated Prototype #1X) used for high-speed handling tests, modified for single-crew operation.
Bu. No. 157992: Thirteenth prototype used to test the Hughes Phoenix Missile System.
Bu. No. 157993: Fourteenth prototype used to test the Hughes Phoenix Missile System.

Chapter Three

The F-14 had a number of unique features that set it apart from any other aircraft in the world. It had a variable swing-wing, an integrated computer and AWG-9 weapons system, and carried the Phoenix missile; all in all, it was possibly the most lethal fighting machine in the world at that time. The F-14 did not have any ailerons, but used differential tail movements, assisted by wing spoilers for roll control. Because the F-14 was virtually spin-resistant under natural conditions, Grumman decide to use this to produce an aircraft with no angle-of-attack restrictions and one that would not depart from controlled flight. The leading edge of the F-14's wing consisted of one full span slat, while the trailing edge was divided into three slotted flaps. The inboard trailing flap was used solely for landings and take-offs. It also had a number of other unique features, none more so than the swing-wing. Also, designed to operate with the swing-wing, there were a pair of 'glove vanes' that came out of the fixed wing glove, situated inboard of the movable portion. As the wings swept back, the vanes went forward at programmed speeds to prevent the centre of the pressure of lift from aft, thus reducing drag. The wing automatically adjusted to the best variable sweep position at any one point in the flight envelope by means of an on-board computer. Under combat conditions, the pilot selected the MSP (Mach Sweep Programme) and the variable sweep wing was under constant automatic control. This feature enabled the F-14 to take three different roles: air superiority, fleet air defence and air-to-ground attack.

The USS *Theodore Roosevelt* (CVN-71) launching her aircraft.

A good example of this was to watch the F-14 break over an airfield in preparation for landing. The wings were swept forward from 68 degrees back to 20 degrees full forward as the airspeed bled off. Once on deck the wings were swept full back to 70 degrees to reduce the amount of space the aircraft took up for ease of parking, as can be seen in the photograph. The variable sweep wing enabled the F-14 to attain speeds in excess of Mach 2 and land at 114 knots. It was claimed that the F-14 could land at 60 knots, but the high angle of attack caused the tail pipes to drag on the deck as it touched down, so it was deemed not to be the best approach for landing.

One of the noticeable shapes on the F-14's fuselage were the rectangular inlets, which were offset to avoid the turbulence generated by the junction of the body to the engine inlet. The two-dimensional horizontal shape of the inlets was the perfect shape for the design of the scheduling ramp. The scheduling ramp was controlled by the Air Inlet Control System (AICS) and moved the ramp up and down as the aircraft's speed increased or decreased so that the air always entered at a subsonic speed.

One major improvement built into the design of the F-14 was the cockpit. The cockpit was placed on the highest part of the fuselage, giving 360-degree visibility to the crew. Prior to this only the North American F-86 Sabre afforded the pilot this luxury. The McDonnell-Douglas F-4 Phantom's cockpit was flush with the top of the fuselage, giving the crew no rearward visibility whatsoever. The thinking behind this was that because of the aircraft's Mach 2 capability as an interceptor, drag would be reduced, and its speed and sophisticated radar system would resolve the problem of any attack from the rear. During the war in Vietnam this proved not to be the case as a number of incidents concerning attacks from the rear were recorded.

The cockpit configuration was designed to be pilot-friendly, as can be seen in the neatness of the instrument layout with two rectangular screens situated in the middle of the instrument panel. The Vertical Display Indicator (VDI) was the primary attitude reference indicator in the F-14A/B and was installed in the upper centre of the pilot's instrument panel. The display is a television-like picture of artificially generated ground and sky texture to form a reference horizon. The viewing area is approximately 60 degrees in elevation and 50 degrees in azimuth, and simulates the view through the front canopy. In theory, this enabled the pilot to fly the aircraft during all visibility conditions without reference to the real world, including

An F-14D of VF-213 (Black Lions) being towed to its parking slot after a mission.

Above: A plane captain cleaning the canopy of an F-14 Tomcat.

Right: An F-14D of VF-2 (Bounty Hunters) being manoeuvred onto the outside elevator aboard the USS *Constellation* (CV-64).

USS *Enterprise* (CVN-65) returning from Saigon.

during take-off. The display consisted of a horizon line, pitch lines, pitch trim markers, fixed bank angle indices, video bank angle markers, and ground and cloud texture elements. The physical centre of the scope indicated the armament datum line of the aircraft.

Immediately below the VDI in the F-14A/B was the Horizontal Situation Display (HSD). This was the pilot's primary navigation display, and also had provisions to display data from the infrared seeker, the TCS system (if installed), or data from the ECM system. In the manual navigation mode, symbols for command course, command heading, TACAN bearing and ADF bearing were displayed. Wind velocity, true airspeed and ground speed were also shown. In the TACAN navigation mode, the alphanumeric symbols were omitted and a deviation bar was added, along with range-to-station.

In addition to electronic displays for viewing flight, navigational and ECM data, the pilot's instrument panel contained armament controls, as well as conventional flight and engine instrumentation. Engine controls, fuel management, auxiliary devices, autopilot, and communications control panels were on the left console. The only significant change in the F-14B front cockpit was modified instrumentation necessary for the F110 engines. The aft cockpit of the F-14A/B was equipped for the NFO and contained no flight controls. This instrument panel contained controls and displays for the AN/AWG-9 weapon control system, and also navigational flight instruments. The data from the AN/AWG-9 radar was displayed to the NFO on a 10-inch tactical information display (TID) and a 5-inch multi-mode Detail Data Display (DDD). An upgraded Programmable Tactical Information Display (PTID) was installed in some F-14BS. This display was generally similar to the MFDs (Multi-Functional Displays) used in the F-14D, and was capable of displaying symbology from LANTIRN pods and digital images from the digital TARPS pod, as well as the normal AWG-9 data.

Armament controls, sensor controls, keyboards and communication panels were located on the left console. The left console also contained controls for the TARPS or LANTIRN pod, as appropriate. The right console contained an ECM and navigation display, ECM controls, data link controls and the IFF panel. The only significant aft cockpit modification in the F-14B was the deletion of the previous threat warning indicators and the inclusion of the AN/ALR-67 display on the right console.

The F-14A/B's display subsystems with their fixed display formats were replaced in the F-14D with displays driven by two identical CV-3916A programmable display processors,

Multiple take-offs from the USS *Theodore Roosevelt* (CVN-71).

which provide flexibility for future system expansion and modifications. Two IP-1514/A Multi-function Displays (MFD) were installed in the front cockpit, one on the centre line below the new IP-1494/A wide field-of-vision Head-Up Display (HUD) and one in the upper right part of the instrument panel. Either the HUD or the centre line MFD was selectable as the primary flight instrument, depending upon flight conditions and the pilot's preference.

The aft cockpit included one MFD in the right-hand vertical console in addition to a 5×7-inch radar digital display (DD) and the existing TID on the centre line. Each MFD contained numerous buttons along its perimeter to be used for menu selection, data entry, and system test initiation. Each MFD had a resolution of 525x875 pixels and could present images generated by the TCS, IRSTS, and eventually LANTIRN, in addition to computer-generated symbology. An expanded keyboard was provided in the aft cockpit for use with the AN/ASN-139 inertial navigation set, the SMS, JTIDS, and other subsystems. The MFDs used by the FSD F-14Ds were monochrome units, although colour units were installed in production aircraft.

Each of the F-14D's three sensors (AN/APG-71, IRSTS and TCS) could operate independently or be slaved to any other of the three sensors. Sensor controls were provided on the DD, the MFDs, the pilot's throttle grip and control stick, and the NFO's sensor hand controller and sensor indicator set. Sensor target symbology and information were displayed on the DD, the TID, the MFDs and the HUD. Additionally, TCS and IRSTS video could be displayed on the DD, TID and the MFDs. LANTIRN data was also integrated into the displays when the precision targeting system was finally installed on the F-14D.

Catapult take-off for the F-14 from the deck of an aircraft carrier differed from that of the Phantom F-4 inasmuch as the F-14 nosegear had a built-in holdback fitting that allowed for a reusable holdback bar. The F-4 used a cable/breakaway expendable dumbbell system, which in effect meant that the cable was looped around the breakaway bar situated inside the fuselage of the aircraft. When the catapult reached its required tension on take-off the bar would break, leaving one half on the deck and the other still attached inside the fuselage of the aircraft to be replaced later. The F-14 holdback however stayed in place and could be used for an estimated 7,500 times before being replaced.

The landing gear of the F-14 was exceptionally strong, as landing on the deck of an aircraft carrier can only be described as a 'controlled crash'. The gear lowered backwards as this allowed it to fall into the airstream and be pushed into its locking position in the event

An F-14B having a catapult shoe fitted to its launching bar.

An F-14 being given
the launch signal.

An F-14D of VF-31
(Tomcatters) about to
launch.

An excellent aerial
shot of Tomcats
launching and being
prepared for launch
from USS *Theodore
Roosevelt* (CVN-71).

Preparing to launch from the USS *Theodore Roosevelt* (CVN-71).

Above: An F-14D being given the signal to launch.

Right: Launch crews giving the launch signal.

An F-14 of VF-101 (Grim Reapers) preparing to launch.

Left: The tailhook being checked on an F-14D of VF-31 (Tomcatters).

Below: An F-14 of VF-101 (Grim Reapers) being readied for launch by the launch director aboard the USS *Enterprise* (CVN-65).

An F-14 of VF-101 (Grim Reapers) being signalled to launch by the launch director from the USS *Enterprise* (CVN-65).

Right: An excellent shot of a launch signal being given.

Below: The launch signal is about to be given to the crew of an F-14 of VF-101 (Red Rippers) aboard the USS *George Washington* (CVN-73). Note the crewman kneeling by the nosewheel!

An F-14 taking off from the USS *George Washington* (CVN-73) while a supply ship is alongside replenishing the stores of the aircraft carrier.

of a hydraulic failure. On touching down, the pilot went on to full power as the nosewheel slammed into the deck at a sink rate of 26 feet per second at a weight of 52,000 lbs. Full power was applied in case the pilot missed the wire and had to take off again.

With the AWG-9 weapon system installed, the Navy virtually had the perfect fighter. The AWG-9 was a Hughes development, and consisted of radar, a computer, cockpit displays and weapon interface. The radar could operate in both pulse and Doppler modes, giving the F-14 four times the range and approximately fifteen times the area coverage of the F4J Phantom, which used the Westinghouse AWG-10. The latest AWG-9 radar could detect fighter targets at a range of over 100 miles, and the TCS (Television Camera System) had been added so that visual identification of targets can be made at long range. The AWG-9 also had the ability to monitor twenty-four targets, classifying them into priorities, while deciding which six to attack simultaneously. It even performed some navigation problems, if required. However, there is one function unique to the F-14 called Data Link. This is a voiceless, two-way communication system that enables the air warfare commander on an aircraft carrier to place an additional eight targets on the NFO's (Naval Flight Officer) display.

The F-14's four main weapons are the AIM-54 Phoenix missile, the Sidewinder AIM-9N missile, the Sparrow III AIM-7F missile and the M-61 rotary cannon. Operating in the pulse Doppler mode, the Phoenix was a radar-homing missile that was semi-active and had a terminal active radar base. It was designed to handle the threat of fighter and bomber aircraft and surface-to-surface missiles. In comparison, the Sidewinder AIM-9N operated over a very short range only. It was derived from the very successful heat-seeking version that was widely used in Vietnam by the US Navy. The early Sidewinders had to be lined up on their targets before they could be fired, but the current ones have SEAM (Sidewinder Expanded Acquisition Mode), which enabled the missile to start tracking its target even before it was launched. This was accomplished by tuning the seeker head on the missile to the aircraft's radar. Although there were two other versions of the AIM-7, the E and the F, the N was deadlier. The AIM-7E was guided by a continuous radar wave only, while the AIM-7F was guided by wave and pulse Doppler. The AIM-7N has an all-aspect capability, which meant that the missile could shoot the target head-on or from the side. The N was also capable of going after high-altitude targets, and had a closer minimum range, which was invaluable.

34

Above: An F-14D coming to an abrupt stop after catching the wire.

Right: An F-14 Tomcat of VF-213 (Black Lions) catching the wire aboard the USS *Theodore Roosevelt* (CVN-71).

An F-14 with arrester hook extended, about to touch down.

Above: An F-14 of VF-31 about to catch the wire aboard the USS *Theodore Roosevelt* (CVN-71).

Left: An F-14B of VF-32 (Swordsmen) about to touch down on the aircraft carrier USS *Harry S. Truman* (CVN-75).

An F-14 of VF-101 (Grim Reapers) catching the wire aboard the USS *Enterprise* (CVN-65).

Above: An F-14 of VF-103 (Jolly Rogers) carrying out a high-speed flypast of the USS *George Washington* (CVN-73).

Right: An F-14 about to make a low-level pass of an aircraft carrier.

Above: An F-14D of VF-31 (Tomcatters) making an 'arrested' landing aboard the USS *John C. Stennis* (CVN-74).

Right: Sparrow air-to-air missiles being loaded onto an F-14 aboard the USS *John F. Kennedy* (CV-67).

The M-61 rotary cannon was internally mounted and capable of firing 6,000 rounds of ammunition per minute. Although it carried only 676 rounds of ammunition, giving nine seconds of actual firing time, its accuracy is staggering. The gun sight is linked to the AWG-9 digital computer, which utilizes inertial and radial inputs. Toward the end of 1971, five F-14As' weapon and fire control systems were reaching the final stages of trials conducted by the Navy and Grumman. The NPE (Naval Preliminary Examination) had been successfully passed and no major problems had been discovered, although problems of a financial nature were beginning to appear on the horizon. Carrier capability trials were held aboard the USS *Forrestal* (CVA-59) in June 1971 and all were successful. In July, the second phase of the NPE took place and, unusually, was separated into two sections, NPE (West) and NPE (East). NPE (West) was held at the Naval Missile Centre and concentrated on the evaluation and testing of the weapons system, while NPE (East) was concerned with the F-14A's aerodynamics.

The first deliveries to the US Navy began in September 1972, coinciding with the Navy Board of Inspection and Survey's final evaluation. The squadron taking delivery, VX-4, was one of three squadrons that accepted all new aircraft, prior to the Navy putting them into full fleet service, for operational tests and evaluation.

The financial problems between Grumman and the Navy finally came to a head in August 1972, when Grumman Chairman and President Clinton Towl told the Navy that if Grumman was not paid an additional $545 million for the final 227 of the 313 F-14as on order, they would have to close their doors. Grumman had sensed this situation coming for the first year after the contract had been awarded to them. They had bid $2,900 million to build 494 aircraft. This number was later increased to 772, and then reduced to 313, which reduced the original quote to $2,426 million just prior to the awarding of the contract. The later quote undercut McDonnell-Douglas's by $100 million. The contract was signed under the Total Package Procurement, which meant that there was a fixed price for the entire package. By 1973 it was becoming increasingly obvious to Grumman that the aircraft could not be built at 1969 prices because of inflation and rising company overheads.

Above: Crews aboard F-14s preparing for launching.

Left: F-14 Tomcats undergoing sea trials aboard the aircraft carrier USS *Forrestal* (CV-59) in 1973.

Maintenance crews working on an F-14 inside the hangar aboard the USS *Harry S. Truman* (CVN-75).

Right: Inside the enormous hangar aboard the USS *George Washington* (CVN-73).

Below: An F-14 undergoing maintenance inside the hangar aboard the USS *Harry S. Truman* (CVN-75).

Above: A perfect example of how to overcome the complex parking arrangements aboard an aircraft carrier.

Left: An F-14A Tomcat of VF-51 (Screaming Eagles).

An F-14 Tomcat of VF-124 (Gunfighters) on a training flight.

Above: An F-14A Tomcat of VF-33 (Starfighters) on the catapult, about to be launched from an unknown aircraft carrier.

Right: An F-14A Tomcat taking off for a test flight from Bethpage, Long Island, New York.

An F-14D Tomcat in the latest grey livery.

Clint Towl wrote to the Deputy Secretary of Defence, David Packhard, explaining the problem. Packhard tried to hold Grumman to the letter of the contract, but Grumman were in a 'sink or swim' situation and to swim, a new contract had to be negotiated. The problem was resolved when Grumman agreed to accept a loss of $205 million on the first 134 F-14As, if the Navy agreed to buy the next fifty aircraft at 1974 prices. The losses were enormous for Grumman, but because the rest of the company was profitable, they were able to survive – but only just. The Navy would continue to procure F-14As up to a total of 334, but there was a pressure to reduce the cost of additional aircraft. One way this was achieved was by reducing the amount of work sub-contracted.

Other problems started to dog the F-14A, the most important being the extremely slow production rate. Two and a half years after the aircraft's initial flight, only twenty-seven F-14As had been built and delivered, and the contractual figure of fifty-four aircraft by the end of 1973 looked totally impossible to meet. Grumman appointed George Skurla to head a new management team to sort out the assembly process and, with only days to spare, they achieved their target. The US Navy took delivery of the fifty-fourth F-14A the day before the Christmas holidays started, a truly spectacular production recovery.

The F-14A made its first public appearance at the 1973 Paris Air Show, where it astounded an enthusiastic and enthralled crowd with a display of low flying at 105 knots, while retaining lateral control. With the wings swept back to 40 degrees, the aircraft pulled 6.5G at 400 knots, and made slow rolls with the wings fully swept back to 68 degrees at 250 knots. It was one of the most impressive performances ever seen at a military/civilian air show anywhere in the world and it placed America back in the forefront of aviation development. It also sent shock waves through the Soviet military hierarchy and made them look again at their own fighter programme. Just after the Paris Air Show, the Shah of Persia (Iran) visited the United States, accompanied by a team of military advisors, with the express purpose of buying the best fighter aircraft available. The previous year, the then President of the United States, Richard Nixon, had visited the Shah and had come back with an agreement to sell the Iranians the F-14 and the F-15. This caused a great deal of comment back in the United States, because the aircraft were not even on the production line, and the agreement would mean selling an American front-line fighter to a foreign government.

The sale went ahead, but the Shah changed his mind about the F-15 and only purchased the F-14. It is thought that the Phoenix missile and the long-range radar system swayed his decision, but the main reason was probably the cost of supporting two totally different systems. Eighty F-14 Tomcats were ordered in two separate purchase agreements of thirty and fifty respectively. Also included in the agreement were 424 Phoenix missiles (although only seventy were actually delivered).

In 1979, the Shah was overthrown and the Imperial Iranian Air Force ceased to exist. Today the Iranian Islamic Revolutionary Air Force has only seven of the original seventy-nine F-14As left, and these at the expense of cannibalising the others (No. 80 is in storage at the Davis-Monthan AFB). The selling of the F-14A Tomcat to a foreign power was to be the first and the last.

During 1974, VF-1 (Wolf Pack) and VF-2 (Bounty Hunter) took delivery of twenty-four F-14As, and in September went on their maiden tour aboard the USS *Enterprise*. Familiarisation and air intercept missions were carried out with great success, but in January 1975 two F-14As were lost in separate incidents. Fortunately, both crews managed to eject safely and were picked up by rescue helicopters, but all the F-14 Tomcats were grounded for inspection. Both crews had said that, prior to ejecting, they had heard a loud bang in the vicinity of the engines, followed by an immediate loss of power. The engines on the remaining F-14s were stripped down and it

Two F-14A Tomcats in Iranian Air Force livery but with US markings to enable flight testing to be carried out at Calverton, New York.

Two Iranian F-14 Tomcats on a test flight prior to being delivered to the Iranian Air Force.

Above: An F-14 of VF-1 escorting an Ilyushin bomber.

Left: An F-14 of VF-2 (Bounty Hunters) accelerating down the deck of the USS *Constellation* (CV-64). One of the escort destroyers can be seen in the background.

The tail section of an F-14 Tomcat of VF-31 (Tomcatters) being recovered from the sea.

The wreckage of an F-14 Tomcat of VF-31 (Tomcatters) being recovered from the sea after crashing.

was decided that the problem was probably due to the fan blades separating from the engine. On closer inspection, it was realised that the quality of the blades was such that they would all have to be replaced. The engine manufacturers, Pratt & Whitney, had subcontracted the manufacture of the blades to another company and put the blame on poor quality control. The inspection of all the aircraft had taken some months and during this time the grounding had been lifted to allow the training programme to continue. The cruise and shakedown exercises for the squadrons continued without further incident, but in July 1975 an F-14 operating from Naval Air Station Oceana suffered an engine explosion. The incident was identical to that involving the aircraft of VF-1. The explosion occurred in one of the engine compartments soon after take-off, but fortunately the crew were able to extinguish the resulting fire and return safely to base. Again, the cause was attributed to the fan blades, with the result that all the F-14s were grounded for further inspection. But, despite these inspections, problems continued to dog the Tomcat, and after the loss of another F-14 through the same reason, it was decided to install an updated version of the TF-30 engine, the Pratt & Whitney TF30-P-14.

The new engine was not to make an appearance until the mid-seventies, so in the meantime all existing aircraft were modified with kits during their standard depot-level maintenance periods at Naval Air Station Norfolk. In the interim, the US Navy were looking for a completely new engine for the F-14A, and watched with great interest as the USAF put the General Electric DFE (Derivative Fighter Engine), later labelled the F-110, through its paces in the General Dynamics F-16 fighter. The engine seemed to be everything the Navy wanted and contracts were drawn up for a marine version of the F-110, the F-110-GE-400. This would be virtually the same as the USAF version – 80 per cent in fact – the difference being that the engine weight would be distributed differently because of

Above: An F-14A carrying out a low-level run at NAS Oceana.

Left: An F-14D lifting off from NAS Oceana on full afterburners.

An F-14D of VF-101 (Grim Reapers) carrying out a low pass at NAS Oceana.

the F-14's centre of gravity. The F-14 also used a different gearbox and accessory-mounting arrangement, because of the size of the engine bays. The F-110 engine had a higher basic thrust and eliminated the need for afterburners on catapult launches. The engine proved to be among the most reliable of all fast jet engines and produced an increase in safety (up to this point, the F-14 had been powered by the TP30-P-414, which had superseded the TP30-P-14, but was replaced by the F-110).

An incident on 11 September 1980 concerning an F-14 of VF-24 (The Renegades) flying off the aircraft carrier USS *Constellation* caused a great deal of concern. Its pilot, Lt Blake L. Stichter, gave this account after the incident:

On 11 September 1980, the aircraft carrier USS *Constellation* was off the coast of Taiwan and steaming northward toward Korea. My wingman and I had made a normal A.M. launch for a routing air intercept mission. We were making runs against each other. They were running on us this time. Just prior to the pass and a couple of thousand feet above my wingy, I rolled the aircraft inverted and bunted the nose to maintain altitude (0 to slightly negative G). Almost immediately the horizontal stabilizer locked (hydraulically) in a nose down or negative G position. One wing rolled up slightly and while still inverted, the aircraft started a turn at a slight climb from 18,000 to 19,000 ft. The aircraft went through approximately 90 degree of turn at -1G, before the nose finally fell through, pointing directly at the South China Sea. Several attempts had been made to right the aircraft, now pointed at the ocean. I continued aft pressure to pull the aircraft out of the dive. Passing 15,000 ft. we had 350 knots and still no nose movement despite repeated yanks on the stick. At approximately 12,000 ft, noting the extreme situation, I took both hands and pulled on the stick in one last-ditch attempt to pull the aircraft out of the dive. With this attempt the stick broke off in my hands leaving me with a stick grip, a few wires and even fewer options.

By this time we were at 10,000 ft and flying at 450 knots. An immediate attempt was made to eject, but by now the aircraft was in a negative G environment again. I had pinned the face curtain handle against the canopy with my helmet and it became physically impossible to get the handle out. I was resolved to ride the aircraft into the water, however for some unknown reason the aircraft began an inverted move out of the dive at

An F-14 making a low pass along the edge of the deck of an aircraft carrier.

A close-up of an F-14 carrying out a high-speed flypast.

An F-14 of VF-2 (Bounty Hunters) making a hard landing aboard the USS *Constellation* (CV-64).

approximately 8,000 ft. I pushed on the stick stub that remained and allowed the aircraft to continue out of the dive and into an inverted climb, completing the backside of an outside loop. The aircraft bottomed out at approximately 4,000 ft at over 500 knots and had sustained between four and six negative Gs. Passing 5,000 ft in the climb, I rolled the aircraft upright and continued to climb. All flight controls functioned normally at this point. A return to the USS *Constellation* with a successful CV landing followed. Over the next several days the aircraft was given a thorough overstress inspection, panels were pulled out and the systems run through, but no weaknesses were found. Additionally all hydraulic components were replaced. The culprit appears to have been air in the hydraulic systems. Grumman, as is obvious, builds a hell of an aircraft.

The F-14A was upgraded to become a new variant, the F-14D. There was in fact, an F-14B (2) and C (1), but these were just odd variants with upgraded engines and electronics and never amounted to anything. Because of the high development costs of aircraft, especially military aircraft, the selection of hardware already being used by the Navy was of primary consideration. This would minimise not only the development costs, but also the technical risk. Plans under consideration in 1988, but cancelled by the Pentagon the following year, called for the incorporating into the F-14D an Infrared Search and Track System (IRSTS); the Joint Tactical Information Distribution System (JTIDS); an Airborne Self-protection Jamming System (ASPJS); the ALR-67 radar warning receiver; and provision for the aircraft to carry Advanced Medium-Range Air-to-Air Missiles (AMRAAM). The real heart of the new F-14D would have been the new AN/APG-71 radar, which could offer a sixfold improvement over the current analogue system by using high-speed digital processing. It would have also introduced single-pulse tracking and digital scan control, enabling it to locate a target precisely within the radar beam. While target tracking, a digital control of the antenna scan pattern would have enabled the radar to take an occasional scan to look for other aircraft operating while in the track-while-scan mode. Two standard AYK-14 airborne computers, each able to perform two million operations per second and providing up to 704,000 words of memory, would have been in the main avionics processors. New multiplex wiring would have made many miles of wiring, and several very complex multi-pin connectors, totally redundant. The digital avionics would have made not only the controls and displays more flexible, but would have cut the cost of integrating new weapons and capabilities considerably. The hardware and software would have made the F-14D's avionics compatible with the F-18 Hornets and A-6E Intruders, allowing greater flexibility.

One piece of equipment that was re-evaluated and updated by the Navy for the F-14D was the TCS (Television Camera System). As far back as 1978, the TCS was evaluated by VF-14 (Tophatters) and VF-32 Squadrons aboard the USS *John F. Kennedy* (CV-67), and by VF-24 and VF-211 Squadrons aboard the USS *Constellation* (CV-64). Because the TCS was a passive system, it was not detectable by any hostile tracking system. This would enable the Tomcat to visually identify its adversary and determine the type of aircraft and armament carried, before the F-14 itself was within identifiable range. Electronically interfaced with the F-14's AWG-9 fire control system, the TCS could also be connected to the AWG-9's radar antenna, giving simultaneous radar/video target capability. The new TCS gave the crew a 10:1 improvement over normal sight, and when closing speeds were measured

An excellent overhead shot of two F-14 Tomcats of VF-14 (Tophatters) showing their folded wings configuration.

Two F-14B Tomcats of VF-32 (Swordsmen) taking off together from NAS Oceana.

An F-14 Tomcat of VF-211 (Checkmates) flying over a mountainous region in a swept-back wing configuration.

in thousands of feet per second, the AWG-9 radar or fire control computer was able to alter the TCS's line of sight to meet it. The AWG-9 radar was later updated to become the AWG-9D, ensuring that the F-14's Phoenix weapon system would remain the primary armament for the US Navy's aircraft.

The development of the F-14 continued to make steady progress with the introduction of various modifications. Then in 1993, due to declining defence budgets, a move to make the F-14s carry out an additional role as a bomber was introduced. Already a multi-mission aircraft equipped with Tactical Air Reconnaissance System (TARS) and Tactical Air

An F-14 Tomcat from the Pacific Missile Test Centre, fully equipped with missiles.

Reconnaissance Pod System (TARPS), it was the only aircraft in the US Navy's inventory at the time able to carry out full reconnaissance missions. The decision to make the F-14 Tomcat carry bombs was of no surprise to Grumman as they had always known that the aircraft had the capability. The US Navy's avionics centre in Indianapolis developed an adapter, the ADU-703, which provided an interface between the weapons rail and the BRU-32 bomb rack. This enabled the F-14 to carry general-purpose bomb loads. The next step was to carry out software modifications which allowed the aircraft to carry air-to-ground weapons, such as CBU-59 antipersonnel/antimateriel cluster munitions, Gator mines, Rockeye cluster bombs and GBU-16 laser-guided bombs.

In 1994 the Navy operated three configurations of F-14 Tomcat, comprising 385 F-14As, sixty-nine F-14Bs (formerly called F-14A+) and fifty-five F-14Ds. At the beginning of 1996, work began to upgrade all F-14 Tomcats, A/B and D versions, with new digital flight control systems.

On 14 June 1996 at NAS Oceana, Virginia, the US Navy presented its fleet commanders with a new F-14D Strike Fighter. This new Tomcat fighter was equipped with a LANTIRN (Low Altitude Navigation and Targeting Infrared for Night) targeting system. The then Secretary of the Navy, John H. Dalton, declared that they were 'sharpening the Tomcat's claws'. The LANTIRN was a combined navigation and targeting pod that allowed the pilot to pinpoint targets day or night, in all weathers, from a greater standoff range than ever before. It also enabled the pilot to deliver not only conventional munitions, but also laser-guided bombs with great precision using an infrared sensor and a laser designator/range finder. The addition of GPS (Global Positioning System), together with an inertial navigation subsystem that inputs independent navigational data, which in turn provided the Strike Fighter with precise steering, range and target bearing information, had increased weapon accuracy to a point never before imagined.

The contract for the system had been awarded to Lockheed Martin in November 1995 and in a remarkable 223 days they completed the building and integration of the specially configured LANTIRN pods for the F-14. The first of the pods rolled off the assembly line on 30 January 1996 and it took only one day to carry out the necessary modifications to the aircraft. After a series of exhaustive suitability and performance tests at the Naval Air Warfare Centre at Patuxent River, Maryland, the aircraft and its new system exceeded all the Navy's requirements. Three weeks of extensive testing aboard the aircraft carrier USS *Enterprise* (CVN-65) gave the project its 'sea legs'.

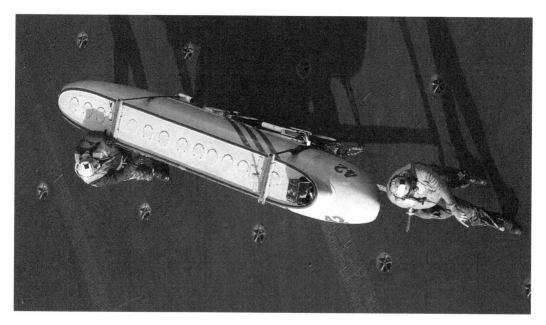

A TARPS pod being wheeled across the deck of the USS *George Washington* (CVN-73) to be fitted onto an F-14 Tomcat.

Above: An F-14 of VF-31 lifting off the runway at NAS Oceana.

Left: An F-14D of VF-101 (Grim Reapers) taking off from NAS Oceana.

An F-14D of VF-101 (Grim Reapers).

Above: An F-14D Tomcat taxiing along the perimeter track at NAS Oceana.

Right: Admiral William Fallon conducting a pre-flight check on an F-14D prior to a familiarisation flight.

An F-14A Tomcat of VF-201 (Hunters) taking off from Calverton, New York.

An F-14 Tomcat on a test flight.

An F-14D making a full afterburner launch.

An F-14 with its tailhook deployed is seen approaching its aircraft carrier.

An F-14D being directed onto the catapult for launching.

The classic pose of a launch officer giving the signal to launch.

An F-14 being directed into its launch position on the catapult.

The last F-14 Tomcat to fly a combat mission. The aircraft is from VF-213 (Black Lions).

During the Gulf War, the US Air Force F-15E and F-16C/Ds used LANTIRN during precision strike operations. In the harsh desert environment, the system was 98 per cent mission-ready throughout the conflict. Thanks to the designers of the F-14 Tomcat, the aircraft was capable of being continuously upgraded.

The F-14 Tomcat was finally retired in 2006, thirty-six years after its first flight – a truly remarkable achievement in aircraft design and adaptation.

Operational History of the F-14 Tomcat

The F-14 made its first combat mission during Operation Frequent Wind in April 1975. The two squadrons involved, VF-1 (Wolfpack) and VF-2 (Bounty Hunters), were deployed aboard the aircraft carrier USS *Enterprise* (CVN-65) with Carrier Air Wing 14. They were tasked with the job of providing air cover during the evacuation of Saigon as well as flying CAP (Combat Air Patrols) over the city. During the CAP missions they were fired upon on a number of occasions by enemy anti-aircraft guns but were not hit. They also did not encounter any fighter aircraft from the Vietnam People's Air Force.

One of a number of incidents that served to highlight the F-14's capability was in August 1981, when two Libyan fighters while over the Gulf of Sidra attacked two Tomcats of VF-41 (Black Aces) from the aircraft carrier USS *Nimitz* (CVN-68). The aircraft, two Soviet-built Sukhoi Su-22 'Fitters', carried out an unprovoked attack by firing air-to-air missiles at the two American aircraft.

The two Tomcat crews were carrying out a CAP (Combat Air Patrol) mission and had been on station for about forty-five minutes, deliberating whether or not to call for a tanker

An F-14A Tomcat of VF-1 (Wolfpack) touching down on the deck of the USS *Kitty Hawk* (CV-63).

An F-14A Tomcat of VF-1 (Wolfpack) from the aircraft carrier USS *Ranger* (CV-61) on patrol.

Post-flight checks on the Sidewinder missiles on an F-14D of VF-2 (Bounty Hunters).

to carry out a mid-air refuelling with the intention of moving to another sector, when two 'hostiles' were spotted on their AN/AWG-9 radar leaving an airfield in Libya. It soon became obvious that the two 'hostiles' were heading straight for them, so the two F-14 Tomcats started to take evasive action. As they did so, the lead Sukhoi Su-22 fired a missile, the bright

Close-up of an F-14 refuelling from an Air National Guard KC-135 tanker over Iraq.

orange flame from under its left wing lighting up the sky around it. Commander Kleeman rolled his aircraft to the left and the missile streaked beneath him and then twisted slightly in the direction of Lieutenant Muczynski's aircraft, but passed harmlessly past. The action of the two Libyan fighters meant that under the rules of engagement the Americans could now engage them. Commander Kleeman closed on the lead Libyan fighter and as it passed in front of him he fired one of his AIM-9L missiles. The missile struck the Sukhoi 22 in the tail, taking it off completely. Seconds later the pilot ejected and started to float down on his parachute. In the meantime Lieutenant Muczynski went after the second Sukhoi. He watched as the Libyan pilot went into a climbing turn and then headed away, but Muczynski had anticipated this manoeuvre and got into a firing position right behind. Launching his AIM-9L missile, he watched it go right up the aircraft's tail pipe and blow off everything up to the wing roots. Fearful of flying into the debris, Muczynski pulled his aircraft into a 6G vertical climb to clear the debris pattern and then rolled his aircraft inverted to watch the Sukhoi, now engulfed in flames, spinning crazily towards the ground. He saw the pilot eject but did not see his parachute deploy. The two F-14s returned to the USS *Nimitz* (CVN-68) while the Libyans began a search for their two pilots.

One hour later two MiG-25 Foxbats were picked up on radar heading towards the USS *Nimitz*. Immediately two F-14 Tomcats were launched to intercept, but the moment they lit up the incoming MiGs with their AN/AWG-9 radars, the two Libyan fighters, on realising they had been targeted, turned away and headed back to Libya.

This incident caused a great deal of consternation among the Soviet military at the time, because it confirmed their worst fears – the F-14 Tomcat was by far superior to anything that they had (although it has to be said the Libyan pilots were not of the same quality as the Soviet and American pilots).

60

This incident was further highlighted in 1985, when four Arab terrorists from the Palestine Liberation Front (PLF) hijacked an Italian cruise ship, the *Achille Lauro*. The captain was ordered to change course and head for Syria. The hijackers then contacted the Egyptian authorities and demanded that Israel release fifty members of the PLO in return for the hostages. The Syrian authorities refused the cruise ship permission to dock and in retaliation for this the hijackers pushed the wheelchair-bound Jewish-American Leon Kinghoffer to the side of the ship and shot him four times. They then threw his body overboard. On being told that they were still being refused permission to dock they threatened to kill again, but they received a message from the PLF saying that no more passengers were to be harmed. The liner docked in Egypt where the four terrorists were released and flown out of Egypt on a chartered Egypt Air Boeing 737 by the Egyptian authorities. On hearing of their intended departure from Egypt, the then President of the United States, Ronald Reagan, ordered the USS *Saratoga*, which was on exercise in the Mediterranean, to launch her aircraft and intercept the airliner with the intention of forcing it to land at the NATO base in Sigonella, Sicily.

The USS *Saratoga* (CV-60) was turned into the wind and seven heavily armed F-14 Tomcats were launched. Two Grumman E-2c Hawkeye surveillance aircraft and four Grumman KA-6D tankers quickly followed them. The whole mission was to be a Grumman affair. The role of the two E-2C Hawkeyes was to locate and track the Boeing 737 and, having done so, establish radio contact with her. Then four of the F-14 Tomcats would take up stations around her, effectively boxing her in, while the three remaining F-14s maintained a position above them as interceptors, in case of interference. The KA-64 tankers were along for refuelling purposes, which were carried out just the once during the mission. The Boeing 737 was located and tracked until it entered international air space, at which point the F-14 Tomcats pounced. At first one of the F-14s flew alongside the 737 and the RIO (Radar Interception Officer), because it was totally dark, actually shone a torch on to the tail of the 737 to confirm it was the right one. Then the remaining F-14s took up positions around the airliner and made their presence known by switching on all their lights. They then contacted the Egyptian pilots by radio, via the E-2C Hawkeye because the airliner had a civilian VHF radio and the F-14s had military ones. Fortunately the E-2C Hawkeye was

USS *Saratoga*.

equipped with both. After acknowledging the instructions given to them, the airline pilots first contacted Tunis, then Greece. Both countries refused them permission to land, leaving them no other choice but to fly to Sigonella, Sicily. At first Sigonella refused them permission to land, but after the captain declared an emergency he was given permission. Once on the ground the Italian Carabinieri surrounded the aircraft and the hijackers were removed from the aircraft and arrested. Not one of the accompanying aircraft landed at the NATO base, but proceeded back to their aircraft carrier.

Considering the crews had only been given two hours' notice of the mission, it was quite a remarkable feat and made even more remarkable by the fact that all the aircraft involved were built by Grumman, emphasising the range of aircraft that the company builds.

On the morning of 4 January 1989, the USS *John F. Kennedy* (CV-67) was sailing toward the eastern Mediterranean Sea for a scheduled port visit to Haifa, Israel. The aircraft carrier was more than 120 miles (190 km) north of Libya and had aircraft operating roughly 80 miles (130 km) north of the country. Aircraft from the USS *John F. Kennedy* included several flights of A-6 Intruders on exercises south of Crete, two pairs of F-14 Tomcats from VF-14 (Top Hatters) and VF-32 (Swordsmen) conducting combat air patrols (CAP), and an E2C Hawkeye from VAW-126 providing airborne early warning and control (EWC). The easternmost combat air patrol station was provided by two F-14s from VF-32 with aircraft call-signs Gypsy 207 (crewed by Commander Joseph Bernard Connelly and Commander Leo F. Enwright) and Gypsy 202 (crewed by Lieutenant Herman C. Cook III and Lieutenant Commander Steven Patrick Collins). Although the *John F. Kennedy* Battle Group was not operating within the contentious Gulf of Sidra and was 600 miles (970 km) away from Rabta, the Battle Group commander believed Libyan concerns of a US attack increased the likelihood of a confrontation. The American aircrews were given a special brief by the battle group commander that emphasised their 'rules of engagement' due to the carrier's proximity to Libya.

At 11.55 local time, the E-2 detected two Libyan MiG-23 Floggers taking off from Al Bumbah Airfield, near Tobruk, and observed them heading north toward the battle group. The F-14s from VF-32 were directed to intercept the MiG-23s, while the F-14s from VF-14 covered the A-6s as they departed to the north. Using their onboard radars, the intercepting F-14s began tracking the MiG-23s when the Libyan aircraft were 72 nautical miles (133 km) away, at an altitude of 8,000 feet (2,400 metres), and travelling at a speed of 420 knots (780 km/h).

A front three-quarter view of an MiG-25 Foxbat taking off.

An F-14A
Tomcat of VF-32
(Swordsmen)
touching down on
the USS *John F.
Kennedy* (CV-67).

An F-14 Tomcat
of VF-32
(Swordsmen)
from the aircraft
carrier USS
John F. Kennedy
(CV-67) with a
Phoenix missile
underneath its
starboard wing.

The USS *Harry S.
Truman* (CVN-75)
being escorted
by the missile
cruiser USS *San
Jacinto*, with two
F-14s from VF-32
(Swordsmen)
giving a
welcoming flyby.

An F-14D of VF-32 (Swordsman) from the USS *Harry S. Truman* (CVN-73) on a reconnaissance mission over Iraq.

Unlike some previous aerial encounters where Libyan pilots were instructed to turn back after detecting an F-14's radar signal sweep their aircraft, the MiG-23s continued to close in on the American fighters with a head-on approach.

As both pairs of aircraft converged, the E-2 and other US eavesdropping assets in the area monitored radio communications between the Libyan aircraft and their ground controllers. The Americans listened to the MiG-23s receive guidance to intercept the F-14s from ground controllers at a radar station in Al Bumbah. This radar station was one of several that were activated along the Libyan coast to support the MiG-23s.

At 11.58, the F-14s made a left turn, away from the MiG-23s, to initiate a standard intercept. Seven seconds later, the MiG-23s turned back into the American fighters for another head-on approach and were descending in altitude. At this point, the F-14 crews began employing tactics that would reduce the effectiveness of the MiG-23s' radars and the 12-mile-range AA-7 Apex missiles they were potentially carrying. The American aircraft started descending from 20,000 feet (6,100 metres) to 3,000 feet (910 metres) to fly lower than the Libyan fighters. The drop in altitude was meant to prevent the MiG-23s from detecting the F-14s by using ocean clutter to confuse their onboard radars. The American pilots executed another left turn away from the Libyan aircraft during the descent. Moments after the F-14s created a 30 degree offset, the MiG-23s turned to place themselves back into a collision course and accelerated to 500 knots (930 km/hr).

The air warfare commander on the USS *John F. Kennedy* gave the American aircrews the authority to fire if they believed the MiG-23s were hostile. The F-14s turned away from the approaching MiG-23s two more times, and each time the American air crews saw the Libyan aircraft turn back toward them for a head-on approach. At 12.00, the Radar Intercept Officer (RIO) in the lead F-14, Commander Leo Enwright in Gypsy 207, ordered the arming of the AIM-7 Sparrow and AIM-9 Sidewinder missiles on the American fighters, after what he determined to be the fifth time the Libyan aircraft turned back toward him.

The American aircrews armed their weapons when the opposing aircraft were less than 20 miles (32 km) away and closing in on each other at a rate of 1,000 knots (1,900 km/h). At a distance of about 14 nautical miles (26 km), the lead F-14 pilot, Commander Joseph Connelly, made a radio call to the carrier group's air warfare commander to see if there was any additional information in regard to the MiG-23s. There was no response to his call. At 12.01 and at a range of 12 nautical miles (22 km), Enwright fired an AIM-7; he surprised Connelly, who did not expect to see a missile accelerating away from his aircraft. The missile failed to track toward its target. At about 10 nautical miles (19 km), Enwright launched a second AIM-7, but it also failed to hit its target.

The MiG-23s continued to fly directly toward the American fighters at 550 knots (1,020 km/h). The F-14s executed a defensive split, where both aircraft made turns in opposite directions. Both Libyan fighters turned left to pursue the second F-14, Gypsy 202. Meanwhile, Connelly prepared Gypsy 207 for a right turn to get behind the MiG-23s as they went after the other American fighter. With the MiG-23s pointed directly at him, Lieutenant Commander Steven Collins, the RIO in Gypsy 202, fired a third AIM-7 from roughly 5 miles (8 km) away and downed one of the Libyan aircraft. After executing a sharp right turn, Gypsy 207 gained a position in the rear quadrant of the final MiG-23. As the Libyan fighter was turning left and at distance of 1.5 miles (2.4 km), Connelly fired an AIM-9 missile, which downed its target. The time was 12.02 when the last MiG-23 was hit by the AIM-9. The F-14s descended to several hundred feet in altitude and departed at high speed back to the carrier group. Both of the Libyan pilots were seen to eject and parachute into the sea, but it is not known whether the Libyan Air Force was able to successfully recover them.

The following day, Libya accused the US of attacking two unarmed reconnaissance planes that were on a routine mission over international waters. Libyan leader Muammar Gaddafi called for a United Nations emergency session to investigate the incident. The US claimed the American aircrews acted in self-defence due to demonstrations of hostile intent by the Libyan aircraft. Two days after the engagement, the Pentagon released photographs taken from the videotapes on the F-14s that, according to US naval intelligence analysts, showed the lead MiG-23 armed with two AA-7 Apex missiles and two AA-8 Aphid missiles. The AA-7 can be either a semi-active radar-homing missile or an infrared-homing (heat-seeking) missile, and it can be fired at another aircraft from head-on. The imagery was used to prove the Libyan fighters were armed and helped support the US position that the MiG-23s were hostile.

It is not known for sure what the actual intent was for the Libyan aircraft on 4 January. Gaddafi could have believed the US was preparing for an attack on the chemical facility in Rabta and ordered his military to see if the aircraft offshore were bombers bound for targets in Libya. The possible reasons for the MiG-23s' flight profile ranged from a deliberate attack against the battle group, to a radio breakdown with ground controllers that led to the Libyan fighters coming into contact with the F-14s. Details released three months after the incident revealed the MiG-23s never turned on their onboard radars, which were needed to guide their AA-7 missiles at maximum range.

During the evacuation of US citizens from Beirut, Lebanon (codenamed Operation Fluid Drive), in 1976, F-14 Tomcats provided CAP patrols in support.

Over the next ten years the F-14 carried out almost constant CAP and photo-reconnaissance missions operating from aircraft carriers cruising off the coast of Lebanon. Then, between 1982 and 1986, when the multinational force combined with US Naval operations was involved in attempting a peacekeeping role, their Tactical Airborne Reconnaissance Pod System (TARPS) missions were used to identify artillery batteries that were firing on the peacekeeping forces, and to provide target intelligence for naval gunfire in support offshore.

In the summer of 1981, F-14s from VF-41 (Black Aces) and VF-84 (Jolly Rogers) performed combat air patrols in support of Freedom of Navigation operations in the Gulf of Sidra. On 18 August 1981, thirty-five pairs of Libyan Air Force fighters and fighter-bombers were intercepted and driven away from the US fleet by F-14s from the USS *Nimitz* (CVN-68) and F-4 Phantom IIs from the USS *Forrestal* (CV-59) on the first day of operations. There was no actual engagement between the two sides. The following day, on 19 August 1981, two Libyan Sukhoi Su-22 (Fitters) opened fire on two F-14As from VF-41 (Black Aces) with an AA-2 Atoll missile. The missile failed to hit either of the F-14s and the American pilots destroyed both Libyan aircraft with AIM-9L Sidewinder missiles. These were the first aerial combat victories in US Navy F-14s and the first for the US since the Vietnam War.

From November 1983 to spring 1984, F-14s from the aircraft carriers USS *Dwight D. Eisenhower* (CVN-143) with VF-142 (Ghost Riders) and VF-143 (Pukin' Dogs), USS *John F. Kennedy* (CV-67) with VF-11 (Red Rippers) and VF-31 (Tomcatters) and the USS *Independence* (CV-62) with VF-14 (Tophatters) and VF-32 (Swordsmen) flew almost daily TARPS missions over Lebanon. The situation aboard the aircraft carriers at the time would have appeared to the layman to be utterly chaotic, but such was the professionalism of the deck crew that aircraft were moved around the crowded deck with ease.

Left: An F-14A of VF-142 (Ghostriders).

Below: An F-14 of VF-102 overflying a Russian Balzam-class intelligence ship.

Above: An F-14 of VF-142 on the catapult aboard the USS *Eisenhower* (CVN-69).

Right: Four F-14B Tomcats in formation.

An F-14 of VF-143 (Pukin' Dogs) launching from the deck of the USS *George Washington* (CVN-73).

Above: An F-14 Tomcat of VF-143 (Pukin' Dogs) and an F/18 Hornet of VFA-131 (Wildcats) about to launch from the USS *George Washington* (CVN-73).

Left: Aerial shot of an F-14 of VF-143 (Pukin' Dogs) about to touch down on the aircraft carrier USS *George Washington* (CVN-73).

An F-14 Tomcat of VF-143 (Pukin' Dogs) catching the wire aboard the USS *America* (CV-66).

Above: F-14 of VF-11 (Red Rippers) carrying out a high-speed pass at NAS Oceana.

Right: An F-14 of VF-11 about to touch down of the deck of the USS *George Washington* (CVN-73) in the Persian Gulf.

An F-14 of VF-11 (Red Rippers) being directed onto one of the four steam catapults aboard the USS *George Washington* (CVN-73).

An F-14 of VF-31 (Tomcatters) accelerating down the deck of the USS *Theodore Roosevelt* (CVN-71).

The crew of an F-14 exiting their aircraft after a mission.

An F-14 of VF-31 undergoing pre-flight checks aboard the USS *Abraham Lincoln* (CVN-72).

A nice side view of an F-14 Tomcat of VF-14 (Tophatters).

Above left: F-14 of VF-32 (Swordsmen) about to launch. Note the compressed nosewheel as the power is applied.

Above right: Ordinance crew preparing to load laser-guided bombs onto an F-14 Tomcat.

An F-14 of VF-32 (Swordsmen) launching from the USS *Harry S. Truman* (CVN-75).

An F-14 of VF-32 (Swordsmen) being readied for launch while a C-2A Greyhound prepares to land.

Ground crews inspecting an F-14 of VF-32 (Swordsmen) on its return from a mission during the Gulf War.

Above: An F-14 of VF-32 (Swordsmen) lifting off the deck of the USS *Harry S. Truman* (CVN-75).

Left: Flight crew of VF-32 (Swordsmen) carrying out a pre-flight check of their F-14 Tomcat.

An F-14B of VF-31 (Swordsmen) refuelling from an Air National Guard KC-135 tanker over Iraq during a combat mission.

An exercise involving the rigging crane that was used to move damaged aircraft.

An F-14D being towed into its parking slot by a 'tug'. This gives a very good idea of the size of this aircraft.

Then on 3 December 1983, two VF-31 F-14As from the USS *John F. Kennedy* came under fire from Syrian anti-aircraft artillery and at least ten surface-to-air missiles were launched against them while they were conducting a TARPS mission. The F-14s were not hit and returned safely to their aircraft carrier. The next day, with all the sites targeted, the Tomcats provided fighter cover for a retaliatory air strike on Syrian positions, destroying all those targeted. On 14 December 1983, Syrian anti-aircraft units fired surface-to-air missiles at another flight of F-14s. The missiles missed and the US responded with naval gunfire from the battleship USS *New Jersey* (BB-62), destroying several anti-aircraft sites.

Despite the anti-aircraft fire and surface-to-air missile attacks, the Syrian Air Force avoided direct confrontation with US forces. There was at least one instance when F-14s engaged, but did not open fire on, Syrian MiG aircraft. Two F-14As from VF-11 (Red Rippers) engaged eight Syrian MiGs over Lebanon; the section was flying cover for a TARPS F-14 and was ready to open fire when the four MiGs that were being targeted decided that discretion was the better part of valour and flew back toward Syria. The other MiGs flew past without engaging.

F-14 Tomcats were actively involved in numerous US military operations directed at Libya between 1980 and 1989. During this period, F-14s shot down four Libyan Air Force aircraft in two aerial engagements over the Mediterranean Sea.

The first of the 'sabre rattling' engagements took place on 21 September 1980, when three F-14s from the aircraft carrier USS *John F. Kennedy* were vectored in to intercept

An F-14 of VF-31 (Tomcatters) climbing away after launching from the USS *Theodore Roosevelt* (CVN-71).

An F-14 of VF-31 being manoeuvred into position on the catapult.

eight Libyan MiG fighters that were attempting to intercept a US Air Force RC-135 on a reconnaissance mission some 200 miles off the coast of Libya. The moment the F-14s arrived on station, all eight MiGs seemed to lose interest and headed back to Libya.

In response to a request from the Somali Government in 1983, two F-14As from VF-102, operating from the USS *America* (CV-66), were tasked with a photo-reconnaissance mission over the Somali port of Berbera in the Gulf of Aden. Reports of pirate activity in the area had prompted the Somali Government to ask for assistance as the practice was becoming rife in the area. Unfortunately no one told the Somali Army of their government's request and the two aircraft were fired on by Somali anti-aircraft units with an SA-2 Guideline, having been mistaken for attacking Ethiopian MiG-23s, but fortunately the F-14s were not hit and were able to complete the mission.

Between 24 July and 14 August 1983, F-14 Tomcats were assigned to the USS *Dwight D. Eisenhower* and were involved in Operation Arid Farmer, the code-name for US military assistance to Sudan, Egypt and the government of Hissene Habre of Chad during the Chadian–Libyan conflict. F-14s performed combat air patrols over waters in and near the Gulf of Sidra during the operation. Several flights of Libyan fighters were intercepted, with neither side opening fire.

During the Freedom of Navigation exercises as part of Operation Attain Document on 24 March 1986, F-14As from VF-102 (Diamondbacks) came under fire from Libyan SA-5 surface-to-air missiles over the Gulf of Sidra, but the missiles did not hit the F-14As. Later the same day, F-14s from VF-33 (Starfighters) intercepted two Libyan MiG-25 Foxbats heading toward the US Naval force. The Libyans were quickly outmanoeuvred by the Tomcats, which got behind the MiG-25s, but the American pilots did not receive permission to open fire. These events and several more surface-to-air launches prompted the US Navy to initiate Operation Prairie Fire. It was the F-14 Tomcats that provided the fighter cover during the operation. The following day an A-7E from the aircraft carrier USS *Coral Sea* attacked and destroyed the SAM (Surface-to-Air Missile) site with an AGM-88A HARM missile.

An F-14 of VF-102 (Diamondbacks) about to catch the wire on the USS *Theodore Roosevelt* (CVN-71.

On 15 April 1986, F-14 Tomcats of VF-33 (Starfighters), VF-102 (Diamondbacks), VF-74 (BeDevilers) and VF-103 (Jolly Rogers) from the aircraft carrier USS *America* (CV-66) participated in Operation El Dorado Canyon, providing fighter cover for the bombers that were carrying out a series of air strikes against targets within Libya. They also carried out CAP missions around the battle group and on two occasions intercepted some MiG-25s that came a little too close.

During the raids on Libya, the F-14 Tomcats' role was to protect the battle group and the aircraft carrying out the bombing raids. The KC-135 tankers were among the most vulnerable while they were carrying out mid-air refuelling of the F-111Bs of the USAF.

During the 'Tanker War' in 1987, F-14 Tomcats of VF-21 (Freelancers) from the aircraft carrier USS *Constellation* (CV-64) were flying escort missions for P-3C Orion reconnaissance aircraft in the Persian Gulf. These were routine missions, but on one occasion, on 8 August, two Iranian F-4s appeared and headed straight for the P-3C Orion. Two F-14s from VF-21 immediately launched three AIM-7 Sparrow missiles, but then, together with the P-3C, left the area before they could see whether or not the missiles had struck home. They were not pursued so it is thought that they did. The US Government played down the incident, not wishing to stir up any speculation. Interestingly enough, the Libyans never mentioned the incident either.

On 18 April 1988, the F-14 Tomcats were once again brought into action during Operation Praying Mantis. This was an attack by US forces in retaliation for serious damage being caused to the guided missile frigate USS *Samuel B. Roberts* by a mine laid in the Persian Gulf by the Iranians during the Iran/Iraq War. The F-14s carried out reconnaissance flights and escort missions during the attacks by US warships.

On 4 January 1989, two F-14As from VF-32, assigned to the USS *John F. Kennedy*, shot down two Libyan MiG-23 Floggers off the coast of Libya. The Libyan fighters appeared to be

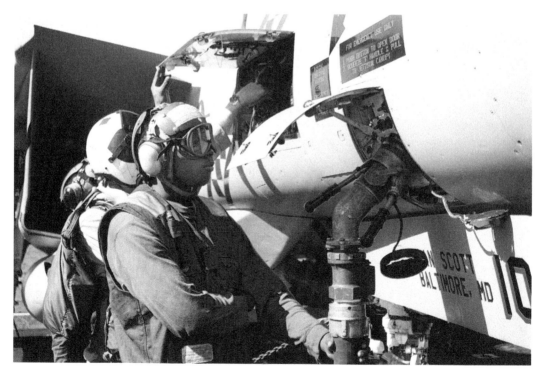

An F-14 of VF-102 (Diamondbacks) being refuelled aboard the USS *Theodore Roosevelt* (CVN-71).

Three F-14A
Tomcats of VF-74
(Be-Devilers).

An F-14 of
VF-103 (Jolly
Rogers)
launching from
the USS *George
Washington*
(CVN-73).

Wing
maintenance
being carried
out on an F-14
of VF-103 (Jolly
Rogers).

Above: An F-14 Tomcat escorting a
Russian Tupolev Tu-95 'Bear'.

Left: Two F-14 Tomcats launching
together in the Persian Gulf.

An F-14 of VF-142 catching the
wire aboard the USS *Eisenhower*
(CVN-69).

manoeuvring for a missile firing position when the Americans concluded they were under attack. The MiG-23s were shot down with AIM-7 Sparrow and AIM-9 Sidewinder missiles.

Operation Desert Shield in 1990 saw the F-14 Tomcat in action once again, operating from the aircraft carriers USS *Dwight D. Eisenhower* (CVN-69) with VF-142 (Ghost Riders) (VF-103 Jolly Rogers) and USS *Independence* (CV-62) with VF-154 (Black Knights) and VF-21 (Freelancers). Their main task was to carry out CAP (Combat Air Patrols) and reconnaissance missions using the TARP system. There were very few aerial targets because the coalition attacks had totally neutralised Iraq's air defence system and grounded the vast majority of Iraq's air force. In total ten F-14 squadrons took part in the war against Iraq. They provided long-range escort protection for attack aircraft and ships and during the short war carried out a total 4,124 sorties.

F-14 aircrews that encountered straggling Iraqi fighter aircraft found that they would disengage once they realised that they were being tracked by the Tomcat's radar and pursued. In one incident, on the first day of Desert Storm, two Iraqi MiG-21s found themselves in just such a position when they came into contact with two F-14s from VF-103. In attempting to escape they ran headlong into four F/A18 Hornets and were shot down.

The only time a F-14 Tomcat was lost to enemy fire was on 21 January 1991 when an F-14B with its pilot Lieutenant Devon Jones and his RIO Lieutenant Lawrence Slade of VF-100 (Jolly Rogers) was shot down by an SA-2 SAM (Surface-to-Air Missile) while escorting bombers on a bombing raid on the Iraqi Al Asad Air Base. Lt Jones was rescued the following day but Lt Slade was captured and held as a prisoner of war until his release on 4 March 1991.

An F-14 of VF-103 (Jolly Rogers) landing aboard the USS *George Washington* (CVN-73).

An F-14 Tomcat of VF-103 (Jolly Rogers) releasing a Phoenix missile during a test on the missile range.

An F-14 of VF-154 (Black Knights) on full afterburner as it leaves the USS *Kitty Hawk* (CV-53).

Despite all their missions during the Gulf War, there was only one air-to-air kill, and that was on 6 February 1991, when an F-14 Tomcat from VF-1 (Wolfpack) shot down an Iraqi Mil Mi-8 helicopter with an AIM-9 Sidewinder missile. There were a number of reasons given for the limited aerial engagements involving the F-14 Tomcat, one reason being that Navy fighters were called off so that other coalition fighters could engage them. One incident, which supports this claim, was when a USAF E-3 Sentry did not inform naval units that two Iraqi Mirage F-1Eqs had flown into the Persian Gulf. Although the F-14s were in a perfect position to engage with them, Saudi F-15s were vectored in to intercept. The US Air Force cited technical and procedural difficulties in passing information and that the E-3 Sentry could not contact the F-14s directly because they were under the radar control of the guided missile cruiser USS *Warden* (CG-18), who in turn said that they were unable to get a clear enough radar picture of the two Mirage fighters to be able to vector in the F-14 Tomcats.

Operation Deliberate Force was launched in August 1995 during the war in Bosnia. F-14 Tomcats of VF-14 (Tophatters), VF-31 (Tomcatters) and VF-41 (Black Aces) from the aircraft carrier USS *Theodore Roosevelt* (CVN-71) carried out strikes in eastern Bosnia on a Serbian ammunition dump using laser-guided bombs – the first time these bombs had been used under combat conditions. The Tomcats also acted as Forward Air Controllers and carried out a number of TARPS (Tactical Airborne Reconnaissance Pod System) missions as well as patrolling the No-Fly Zones in Iraq. VF-41 logged over 600 combat hours during August and September.

It was because of the failure of the Iraqis to cooperate with the United Nations Weapons Inspectors that Operation Desert Fox was launched on 16 December 1998. The aircraft carrier USS *Carl Vinson* (CVN-70) was sent to the area and almost immediately VF-32 (Swordsmen) F-14 Tomcats carried out a night raid. During the three-day operation, VF-32 Tomcats dropped a total of 111,054 lbs (50,373 kg) of munitions during sixteen strike missions. VF-213 (Black Lions), also from the USS *Carl Vinson*, dropped the first GBU-24 Paveway III laser-guided bombs using the LANTIRN system. The squadron carried out seventy missions logging over 615 combat hours as well as forty-five reconnaissance missions, in which they imaged more than 580 targets. During one of the reconnaissance missions two of the Tomcats, armed with Phoenix missiles, came into contact with two Iraqi MiG-25s. As they approached the Tomcats launched their missiles at the incoming MiGs but the two Iraqi aircraft beat a very high-speed retreat and the missiles missed.

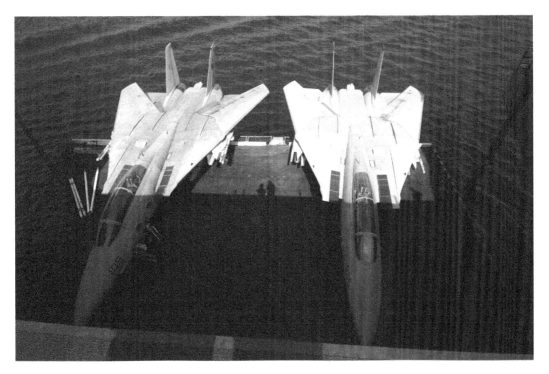

Two F-14 Tomcats of VF-31 (Tomcatters) being lowered on a side elevator to the hangar below deck on the USS *Theodore Roosevelt* (CVN-71).

Above: An F-14D Tomcat about to touch down on the USS *Theodore Roosevelt* (CVN-71).

Right: F-14s being lined up for launch.

With the war in Afghanistan suddenly erupting, the F-14 Tomcats' special skills and weapons were soon in demand. The USS *Enterprise* (CVN-65) with aircraft from Carrier Wing 8, VF-14 (Tophatters), VF-41 (Black Aces), VF-102 (Diamondbacks), VF-211 (Checkmates) and VF-213 (Black Lions), dropped more than 1,334,000 lbs (605,000 kg) of bombs on a number of targets.

These were long-range missions as the aircraft carriers were patrolling in the Indian Ocean. As well as carrying out bombing raids on selected targets, the F-14s were tasked with escort, ground support and reconnaissance missions. They were joined by F-14s from the USS *Dwight D. Eisenhower* (CVN-69), comprising Carrier Air Wing 7 – VF-11 (Red Rippers), VF-103 (Jolly Rogers) and VF-143 (Pukin' Dogs) squadrons – who dropped 64,000 lbs (29,000 kg) of bombs, including the first JDAM (Joint Direct Attack Munition) bombs in combat. This is a guidance kit that converts conventional unguided bombs into all-weather 'smart' bombs.

Above: USS *Enterprise* (CVN-65) in the Gulf.

Left: An F-14 of VF-211 (Checkmates) undergoing a final check before launch from the USS *Enterprise* (CVN-65).

Above: An F-14 of VF-211 (Checkmates) carrying out a night launch aboard the USS *John C. Stennis* (CVN-74) during the Iraq War.

Right: An F-14D of VF-213 (Black Lions) about to touch down on the deck of the USS *Harry S. Truman* (CVN-73) in rough seas.

An F-14A Tomcat of VF-213 (Black Lions).

An F-14 being directed into launch position.

Above: The ready to launch signal being given
to the crew of an F-14D Tomcat.

Left: The launch director guiding an F-14
Tomcat on to the catapult.

Above: An F-14 launching from an aircraft carrier. This shows how cluttered the deck can become during an operation.

Right: An excellent shot of an F-14 clearing the deck after launch.

Maintenance crew of VF-11 (Red Rippers) giving one of their F-14 Tomcats a wash and brush up.

The CAG (Commander Air Group) aboard the USS *Harry S. Truman* (CVN-73), watching launch procedures during the Iraq War.

An F-14 of VF-103 (Jolly Rogers) banking away from a USAF KC-135 tanker after refuelling.

An F-14 of VF-103 (Jolly Rogers) launching from the deck of the USS *John F. Kennedy* (CV-67).

During their ten-week deployment in Afghanistan, VF-213 logged over 500 combat missions, 2,600 combat hours and dropped 435,000 lbs (197,000 kg) of bombs. They also dropped the first bombs during Operation Freedom. VF-102 logged more than 5,000 combat hours – the highest of any F-14 squadron during the operation – and dropped 50,000 lbs (23,000 kg) of bombs. The arrival of VF-103 (Jolly Rogers) in June 2002 increased the firepower of the coalition forces but they did not get to drop any bombs during the short time they were there. VF-211 carried out 1,250 missions, logging 4,200 combat hours, and dropped over 100,000 lbs (45,000 kg) of bombs. Not all the squadrons were involved in pure bombing raids; VF-14 led more strikes and gave more fighter cover than any other squadron, but still managed to drop 174 laser-guided bombs totalling 179,324 lbs (81,340 kg) and twenty-eight AGM-65 Maverick missiles. VF-41 dropped more than 200,000 lbs (9,100 kg) of bombs, of which 202 were laser-guided. They had a remarkable 82 per cent level of accuracy – the highest ever achieved by the US Navy.

Operation Iraqi Freedom saw the F-14 squadrons in action again in 2003 against Saddam Hussein's forces. Aircraft from the USS *Kitty Hawk* (CV-63), comprising VF-2 (Bounty Hunters), VF-31 (Tomcatters), VF-32 (Swordsmen), VF-154 (Black Knights) and VF-213 (Black Lions) squadrons, flew a total of 2,547 missions and dropped 1,452 bombs with the loss of one aircraft and that was from engine failure. The squadrons were also tasked with supporting ground troops and acting as Forward Air Controllers for other strike aircraft. On one mission an F-14D equipped with TARPS (Tactical Airborne Reconnaissance Pod System) dropped four Mark 82 bombs on Saddam Hussein's Presidential yacht *Al-Mansur* (*The Victor*).

The last three years of the F-14s active service was spent in the Persian Gulf with VF-31 (Tomcatters) and VF-213 (Black Lions) supporting the US ground troops in Iraq. During this time the two squadrons amassed 1,163 combat missions with a total of 6,876 flight hours, during which they dropped 9,500 lbs (4,300 kg) of bombs while carrying out surveillance, reconnaissance and support missions. However it was finally time to retire the Grumman F-14 Tomcat, and say goodbye to one of the finest attack aircraft ever built.

F-14Ds of VF-31 (Tomcatters) preparing for a multiple launch.

An F-14 Tomcat
flying past the
bridge of the USS
Theodore Roosevelt
(CVN-71).

An F-14 about to
launch from the
USS *Theodore
Roosevelt* (CVN-71).
Note the blast
barrier raised
behind the aircraft.

Air-to-air refuelling
of an F-14 from
a USAF KC-135
tanker.

An F-14 of VF-32 (Swordsmen) leaving the deck of the USS *Harry S. Truman* (CVN-75).

An F-14 of VF-32 (Swordsmen) catching the wire aboard the USS *Harry S. Truman* (CVN-75).

An F-14 of VF-154 (Black Knights) about to launch from the USS *Kitty Hawk* (CV-53). Note the compressed nosewheel as the power goes on.

An F-14 of VF-154 (Black Knights) being hoisted aboard the USS *Ronald Reagan* (CVN-76) for the aircraft carrier's commissioning ceremony.

An F-14 of VF-213 (Black Lions).

A perfect silhouette shot of an F-14 over the Persian Gulf.

F-14 Tomcat Model Variations

YF-14A: The prototype F-14 Tomcats, fourteen of which were built for research and development. The first crashed while on a second test flight over Calverton, both members of the crew ejecting safely. They were powered by two Pratt & Whitney TF30-P-412A turbofan engines.

F-14A: Production model fitted with AWG-9 radar, the AIM-54, AIM-7 and AIM-9 missiles and powered by two Pratt & Whitney F401-P-400 turbofan engines.

F-14A: Forty-eight F-14s were modified into photo-reconnaissance aircraft by installing TARPS (Tactical Airborne Reconnaissance Pod System) beneath the rear fuselage in a container.

F-14B: Two F-14As installed with improved Pratt & Whitney F401-P-400 engines.

F-14C: This was destined to be an F-14B with improved avionics, but it never materialised.

F-14+: A basic F-14A, but with two General Electric F110-GE-400 engines. The first in a two-step programme.

F-14D: Also known as the Super Tomcat, the F-14D was powered by two General Electric F110-GE-400 turbofan engines. It was fitted with an advanced digital processing air-to-air radar, state-of-the-art digital avionics and a passive detection infrared search and track system. The first test flight took place in November 1987.

Grumman F-14 Tomcat
Technical Details

Type: Interceptor Fighter
Wing Span Extended: 64 feet 2½ inches.
Wing Span Maximum Sweep: 38 feet 2½ inches.
Wing Span Maximum Oversweep: 33 feet 3½ inches.
Wing Area: 62 feet 8½ inches.
Max. Speed: Mach 2.4 (1,591 mph).
Rate of Climb: 30,000 feet per minute.
Service Ceiling: 50,000 feet.
Weight – Cold Combat: 39,762 lbs
Weight – Catapult: 74,348 lbs
Engines: Two Pratt & Whitney TF30-P-412As or 414
                                turbofans each rated at 12,500 lbs dry and
                                20,900 lbs with afterburners.
Armament: Sidewinder missiles, Sparrow missiles,
                                M-61 machine gun and Phoenix missiles.
Crew: Two – Pilot and Avionics and Weapons Officer.

List of F-14 Squadrons

VF-1 Wolfpack
VF-2 Bounty Hunters
VF-11 Red Rippers
VF-14 Tophatters
VF-21 Freelancers
VF-24 Checkertails
VF-31 Tomcatters
VF-32 Swordsmen
VF-33 Tarsiers
VF-41 Black Aces
VF-51 Screaming Eagles
VF-74 Bedevillers
VF-84 Jolly Rogers
VF-101 Grim Reapers
VF-102 Diamondbacks
VF-103 Sluggers
VF-111 Sundowners
VF-114 Aardvarks
VF-124 Gunfighters
VF-142 Ghostriders
VF-143 Pukin' Dogs
VF-154 Black Knights
VF-201 Hunters
VF-211 Checkmates
VF-213 Black Lions

Abbreviations

ADF	Automatic Direction Finding
AICS	Air Inlet Control System
AIM	Air Interceptor Missile
ATE	Advanced Technology Engine
AWG	Airborne Weapons Group
CNO	Chief of Naval Operations
DCNO	Deputy Chief of Naval Operations
DD	Digital Display
ECM	Electronic Counter Measures
HSD	Horizontal Situation Display
HUD	Heads-Up Display
IFF	Identification Friend or Foe
IRSTS	Infra-Red Search and Track System
JTIDS	Joint Tactical Information Distribution System
LANTIRN	Low Altitude Navigation and Targeting Infrared for Night
MFD	Multi-Functional Display
NACA	National Advisory Committee for Aeronautics
NASA	National Air and Space Administration
NFO	Naval Flight Officer
PTID	Programmable Tactical Information Display
R&D	Research and Development
RDTE	Research Development and Test Evaluation
TACAN	Tactical Air Navigation System
TARS	Tactical Air Reconnaissance System
TARPS	Tactical Airborne Reconnaissance Pod System
TCS	Total Control System
TID	Tactical Information Display
VDI	Vertical Display Indicator
VFX	Navy Fighter Experimental